ISBN 978-1-334-36315-3
PIBN 10736762

1 MONTH OF
FREE
READING

at

www.ForgottenBooks.com

By purchasing this book you are eligible for one month membership to ForgottenBooks.com, giving you unlimited access to our entire collection of over 1,000,000 titles via our web site and mobile apps.

To claim your free month visit:
www.forgottenbooks.com/free736762

English
Français
Deutsche
Italiano
Español
Português

www.forgottenbooks.com

Mythology Photography **Fiction**
Fishing Christianity **Art** Cooking
Essays Buddhism Freemasonry
Medicine **Biology** Music **Ancient**
Egypt Evolution Carpentry Physics
Dance Geology **Mathematics** Fitness
Shakespeare **Folklore** Yoga Marketing
Confidence Immortality Biographies
Poetry **Psychology** Witchcraft
Electronics Chemistry History **Law**
Accounting **Philosophy** Anthropology
Alchemy Drama Quantum Mechanics
Atheism Sexual Health **Ancient History**
Entrepreneurship Languages Sport
Paleontology Needlework Islam
Metaphysics Investment Archaeology
Parenting Statistics Criminology
Motivational

A BOOK OF POEMS.

With respects from the writer to the reader. May this book be cast abroad, trusting that its mission will be attended with good results.

Sincerely yours,

LULU EVERTS.

Copyrighted 1917.

By LULA EVARTS.

Printed by Halbert R. Stephens,
Oklahoma City, Okla.

June, 1917

Through the kind introduction of "Buffalo Bill", W. F. Cody, I sent these poems to the editor of Merry War, Clinton, Iowa. Mr. Benjamin F. Gilbert, who was born May 22, 1822, at Chambersburg, Penn. Mr. Gilbert was Buffalo Bill's first school teacher, at Peases Grove, Scott County, Ia. Fifty years had elapsed when B. F. Gilbert happened to be in Rock Island, Ill, where Buffalo Bill's Wild West Show was playing. He went to the performance, met Buffalo Bill and had a long personal talk with him. Mr. Cody had recognized his old school teacher on sight. He had been a mere lad of six when he went to school under Mr. Gilbert. Though over fifty years had elapsed, he remarked as he laid his hand on Mr. Gilbert's head and shook his hand with a firm grasp, "I have traveled all over Europe, have shaken hands with great Monarchs and Queens, and with Presidents of the United States, but one firm grasp from that dear old hand that taught me my A B C's does me more good than anything in the world." With tears rolling down his cheeks when he bade his old school master good bye, he remarked: "God bless you, I hope we meet again."

After his old friend had started to leave, he called him back, wiping the tears from his eyes and began laughing. "Whatever became of your boy, Dewese, that I played with, the one that swallowed the bullet?" "Oh!" remarked Mr. Gilbert, "the bullet didn't hurt him, he is still alive, the last time I heard, and has raised a large family, living now at Beatrice, Nebraska."

This is a true statement and can be vouched for by the Editor of Merry War, Clinton, Iowa.

Benjamin Franklin Gilbert died at Davenport, Iowa, Aug. 5, 1904.

WOMAN.

By W. R. Austin.

There is the idle woman,
Who lives in town,
That nothing will please,
But to dress like a clown.
She clatters and chats
About ribbons and hats
And anything else would bring forth a frown.
But if to her face you'd bring forth a smile,
Get her a fashion plate,
And talk about the style,
And tell her she's right up to date,
She'll be the happiest woman in the state.
But then if you wish a few fights,
Just change your position and oppose woman's
    rights.
And soon you'll hear,
The gossips report,
She's gone to a judge
And haled you into court.
Then comes the busy woman,
Who lives on the farm,
And cares little for fashion or style,
But takes great pride
In the look of the farm,
And the pleasures of home,
That make hubby smile,
To the pleasures of home' she's wide awake.
So she bakes her own bread, pies and cake
And has no time for the gossips from town
Who advise her to make of herself a clown.
For she's busy all day with home-making affairs,
That tend to make pleasures of hubby's cares,
And that keep love long ago won,
Instead of the gossip that's done.

LOVELY MARY.

By W. E. Austin and Lulu Evarts.

Copyrighted by Lulu Evarts.

On her cheeks the roses bloom,
Bonny blue in each bright eye,
She'll be a beauty soon,
With lots of smiles and not a sigh,
With rosette lips so sweet to kiss,
And pearly teeth so white,
The first of which I'd never miss,
If I but had the right.
Her bonnet's always trimmed in blue,
And rouge upon her face,
A shiny buckle on her shoe,
   Her frocks all trimmed in lace,
   She'll win the prize of ardent love,
With good cheer never weary,
From those who love a gentle dove,
For such is Lovely Mary.

WRECKED ON BOARD THE BARK OF LOVE
By W. F. Gilbert.

Cast upon life's stormy sea,
Wrecked on board the bark of love,
Are there no joys for me,
Until I reach my home above?
Alas, I'm sad and forlorn,
From my loved ones cast away;
Ah! How good never to have been born
To meet sad disappointment and sore dismay.
But I hope some day to find,
'Ere life shall cross death's dark glen,
My loved ones to be more kind,
And permit me to be with them,
And in their joys and pleasures mingle,
To rest my aching heart,
To hear their merry laugh that tingles,
All these sad hours we are apart.

FOR THE KING OR KNAVE.

(A War Song).

By G. W. Gilbert.

How many who wonder why,
Our soldiers go to battle and to die,
For mere order of a king or knave,
Only to fill a warrior's grave.
When all is said and done,
And the soldier's race is run,
What more can be said,
For his obedience, he is dead.
For his king and crown,
He went to the front,
And was there cut down.
To him who is slain,
For some other's fame,
The world has no pleasures more;
For him who on the battle field, spilled his gore,
But why should in wonder attempt to tell,
The horrors and the glories of those who in
battle fell.

IN RAPTURE SUBLIME.

(Dedicated to Little Polney).

Sweet Little Polney has a sweet little face,
And eyes of azure blue,
An agile form full of grace,
A heart ever fond and true,
And a head of silken curls,
That every one first exclaims,
"Oh! What a pretty little girl!"
Because the face wears a smile of bloom,
The fact of the matter is,
The little silken head is a boy,
And with his childish prattle,
Is his mother's pride and joy.

A DAISY IN THE DELL.

Written July 1, 1914.

I asked a daisy in the dell,
Which brightens all that is lovely in life,
To give me truth that truth might be,
My guiding star to everlasting life.
"Ah," replied the daisy,
"I'll give you truth,
For truth is reason,
And all things come in season;
And life is like a dream,
And not what it seems.
For soon we enter life,
With all its joys and strife—
Too soon we die,
Nor learn we the reason why,
But blighted in our fondest hopes,
We return to that from which we came—the
Unknown."

A REFLECTION.

By J. W. Evarts, Written in 1852.

Ah, yes, it is pleasant,
To view a bright star,
Enthraled by its lustre sublime,
Transiently pleasant,
But sweeter by far,
When leisurely I may recline
In the warm fragrant groves
Where the light heart roves,
And Cupid is jester for Time.
Let Angels' bright wings
Fan deftly the brow
Of the spirit who sings of friendship's vow
While I worship at friendship's shrine,
Bringing treasures from friendships of mine.
And I quaff the sweet wine,
Of the spirit divine,
While the Angels have gone
To their palace of song.

THE OLD WOODEN ROCKER.

Mother, dear mother,
Come kiss me good night,
And sing me a song
That was my delight,

Chorus.

Of the old wooden rocker.
That dear old rocker
That rocked to and fro,
That rocked me to sleep long ago.

Many a night my mother
Rocked me, a babe, to sleep,
Now mother has gone
And left me alone to weep

Chorus.

By the old wooden rocker.
That dear old rocker
That rocked to and fro,
That rocked me to sleep long ago.

Oh, mother, dear mother,
Your fond memory I keep,
As o'er my infancy
You rocked me to sleep.

Chorus.

In the old wooden rocker
That dear old rocker
That rocked to and fro,
That rocked me to sleep long ago.

That old wooden rocker;
How dear to my heart,
As memories round me creep,
Of mother who rocked me to sleep.

Chorus.

In the old wooden rocker,
That dear old rocker,
That rocked to and fro,
That rocked me to sleep long ago.

Many are longing tonight,
As the shadows creep,
For some dear mother
To rock them to sleep.

Chorus.

In the old wooden rocker
That dear old rocker
That rocked to and fro,
That rocked them to sleep long ago.

DREAM, OH DREAM, OF ME AND MINE.

By J. W. Evarts (Written July 1, 1898).

Why do I love? Why do the sky and sea
In whirling act, embrace and dance with glee?
Why light descend, it's heat to lave
Down in the clear and deep blue wave?
Why birds sail far on airy wings
And mate in rapture while they sing?
Can'st tell, sweet one, why blooms the rose?
Why tired life seeks heart's repose?
Then, pretty darling, you can tell
Why my heart loves you so well.
Ah! were I but a bird of wing,
I'd light nearby and softly creep ·
Close by your ear and gently sing
My darling fast asleep,
And whisper, dearest, "I love you,
Pretty darling. Love me too.
Dream of me till mating time,
Dream, oh! dream of me and mine."

I LOVE YOU—DO YOU LOVE ME?

There's a girl in Oklahoma City,
They say she's very witty.
She wrote some lines,
Once upon a time
And here's the way it rhymes.
I love you—do you love me?
If you do, just say so
And we'll be married, honey.
But I ain't got much money,
But what care we, honey,
We'll own our own sweet home.
I don't care about your money,
It's your love, I want, honey,
I'll marry you when you say so,
And we'll be married on our own home sweet
    home.
If we ain't got much money,
We can shoo flies and eat honey.
Ain't that funny? It won't take much money
To keep you and I, honey,
If we own our own sweet home.
Don't marry for money,
But take my advice,
Marry for love,
And live in your own sweet home.
Go search the wide world over,
You'll find no place,
Be it ever so humble,
Like your own sweet home.

DECLINING YEARS.
By J. W. Evarts.
Written Feb. 19, 1852.

Music sweetens and brightens
All that is lovely in life
And lends pinions to our fondest hopes,
It cheers the toiler in the struggle of life,
Inspires courage in heroic deeds,
Buoys the soul towards richer inspirations,
Comforts humanity through declining years.

MY MOTHER'S CHAIR.

There is in our home,
A vacant chair,
A form we'll always miss,
'Tis the image of our mother,
God bless her, we love her,
For we'll never find another
Who can take the place of mother.
We will not forget our mother,
Though she sleep in silent tomb,
Her sweet face we'll never see again
Until we meet in Heaven.
Her picture hangs upon the wall,
Her vacant chair stands near,
But the sweetest of all
Is the memory of our mother.

MY TRUE LOVE.

I shall not forget the day
My true love was laid to rest
With a rose on her breast.
It was in the month of June
When roses are in bloom.
Oh! the tears I could not hide
When I pressed my lips
To her cold, icy finger tips.
Oh! the grief, the tears we cannot hide,
When we bid our loved ones farewell.
Though we have hopes for the spirit that's gone
    to dwell
In the Promised Land,
Where we are told that Angels in robes so white
Will bid our loved ones a welcome to a home
    above,
Where love, music and song shall be a delight
    to their ear,
Then what a glorious sight, if the story be true
That our loved ones in robes so white
Will see the golden gates ajar,
And the glad tidings of the Angels
To bid them welcome to a mansion in the sky,
Where they'll never say good-bye.

WHERE IS HEAVEN, GRANDMA DEAR?

By Prof. Chas. J. Keesee.

Grandma, I am growing tired,
But before I go to sleep,
Come where breezes soft are blowing,
While the nearer shadows creep.
Are the stars, so still and saint-like,
Heaven's windows, Grandma dear?
And are angels looking through them
At us in the garden here?

Chorus.

Where is Heaven, Grandma dear?
Is it very far away?
And if I should leave you here,
Could I reach there in a day?
Will I have an Angel playmate,
Same as little children here,
No one cross and none to tease me?
Where is Heaven, Grandma dear?

Guess the sky is one big curtain,
Really, I believe, don't you?
And the stars are only places,
Where some one has broken through,
But I never could quite make out
How I'll reach so high.
Can I get to Heaven,
When I have no wings to fly?

Chorus.

Where is Heaven, Grandma dear?
Is it very far away?
And if I should leave you here,
Could I reach it in a day?
Will I have an Angel playmate,
Same as little children here,
No one cross and none to tease me?
Where is Heaven, Grandma dear?

CHILD OF MERCY.

Sweet Allah Nook,
A maiden fair,
Fair as ere the sun shone on,
Dark brown were her eyes,
All golden her curls,
And sweet she did look
As she wandered by a brook
With a necklace of pearls,
O'er meadows and hills
She softly stepped,
With her blue checked apron,
Gathering flowers
As she went on,
Her heart in ecstacy
Beat with a thrill
When at last she came
To a little house on a hill.
"This little blue house
Is my home," quoth she,
"This dear little house
That stands on a hill,"
As she came near the cottage door
Where the roses climb the sweetest,
And welcomed her there.
But her dear old dad, who was so glad
As he went to meet his orphaned child,
"Where hast thou been," quoth he,
Though his hair was white as snow,
And his step was slow,
As they went home together.
Then with dainty finger tips, just like pearls,
She swung her bonnet by her side on a bright
    summer's day,

While the gentle breezes softly tossed her curls.
Then her answer came
While she listened to the robins' song so gay,
O'er meadows and hills,
She softly said in her child-like glee,
When she noticed her father's grave, calm, sad
    face,
And half-shut eyes,
Then with her blue checked apron,
She wiped the tears from his soft blue eyes,
Then looking very sad, her answer came:
    "What makes you cry?
Look here, dad, I gathered these flowers for
    you."
As he took the flowers from her soft white hand,
Then his answer came, "I wondered where thou
    wast, my child,
As you whiled so many happy hours away;
Alas, you were not at home—I pray you stay
With your poor old dad, so old and gray,
In this little blue house,
This dear little house
That stands on a hill."
"I'll never leave thee, my dear old dad,
You look so sad since mother died, "she softly
    sighed,
As she seated him in his old arm chair.
Then to his heart's delight,
She sung him many a lullaby,
And soon he was fast asleep on a summer's day,
As his old house dog lay at his feet.
"Oh! My father, as you sink in dreams, low,
    sweet and clear,
Let my voice be near.
Let your aged hand in mine be pressed,
Let your snow-white beard descend on your
    breast.
Let my head be pillowed on your breast."

YOUTH AND OLD AGE.

Once I was young and handsome and gay, so
    they say,
My cheeks were like two red roses, I'm told,
That bloomed on a summer's day.
My hair was black as jet could be; my eyes
    were, too,

But now that I am getting old and gray
I feel life is fading fast away,
When I was young, handsome and gay,
I never dreamed what it was to be old and gray,

But now that I'm feeble, old and gray,
And I cannot see my way,
I'm told that I must go
O'er the hills to the poor-house not far away.

When fortune and kindred gathered around me,
And young swains smiled upon me,
I never dreamed then what it was
To be feeble, old and gray,
And that some day to the poor-house I would go.

But now my fortune has dwindled away,
And my friends have departed, too.
I'm told I must go over the hills
To the poor-house not far away.

When I was young, handsome and gay,
I lived in a mansion grand
And never dreamed then what it was
To be feeble, old and gray,
And that some day, over the hills
To the poor-house I would go.

But now my beauty has faded away,
And here I stand. I'm feeble, old and gray
And on my way, over the hills to the poor-house
Not far away.

THE LITLE WINDOW.

I like the little window
When the sun peeps in at noon.
I like to sit in my easy chair
And smoke my pipe of clay,
And pass the merry hours away
While I watch the children romp and play.
I like to see the baby
As he rolls and tumbles on the floor,
While Lenore, she hides behind the door.
'Tis fine, to see the boys play ball,
For that's their joy and fun.
I like to see them skip,
I like to see them fall
All around the room,
When the sun peeps in at noon.
I love fair Alice,
With big blue eyes and golden hair,
As she plays on the floor,
Making dresses for her dolls,
While her brother, Charles,
Plays at the open door,
With his marbles rolling on the floor.
When the sun peeps in at noon.
Then comes the fun, we, old and young,
Begin to hop and dance
All around the room,
When old Uncle Ephraham begins to play
The old Virginia reel
While sweet little Nell at the cottage door
Is turning the spinning wheel,
When the sun peeps in at noon.
We like to smell the fine fat possum,
Boiling in the pot,
With sweet 'taters all around,
That would invite any coon a mile around
When the sun peeps in at noon.
We, old and young, we like to see the turkey
   trot
We like to see him strut,

We like to see the old bob-tailed rooster
When he titters on the gate,
We like to see old Grover,
When he wags his tail upon the floor,
We like to see Uncle Ephraham,
When he "Hangs up de fiddle and de bow,"
We like to see Mariah when she sweeps the floor
We like to hear the tick of the old brass clock
As it hangs upon the wall,
When the sun peeps in at noon.

SHE'S THE GIRL FOR ME.

Beneath her chapeau
All trimmed in lace,
As she walks with a gentle manner,
So full of grace
All dressed sublime
I know she'll be mine
As she quaffs with me
The flowing chalice,
The nectar's sweet wine,
She's the girl for me,
Sweet Anna Bell.
As she wanders to and fro,
Gathering daises in the dell,
She says she'll be mine
And love no one but me,
My own true love,
Sweet Anna Bell,
As she quaffs with me
The flowing chalice,
The nectar's sweet wine.

BEAUTIFUL EYES.

Ah! love first finds beauty
In a woman's eye,
For she becomes an ardent companion
When she has a fine disposition.
But, oh! such a strange sensation
When she looks at you with sweet surprise
For she knows she's won the prize.
For there's no beauty that shines like a woman's
    eye,
Such beautiful eyes,
Just like azure skies,
They surely hypnotize,
When they look at you
With sweet surprise,
For love and beauty
Shine in a woman's eyes.

WHEN THE WAR IS OVER.
(To Mr. Huntington).

When the war is o'er
Many a longing heart
Will beat with joy,
When the war is o'er.
Many a longing heart will shed a tear
When we soldier boys,
In our uniforms of blue,
With the Stars and Stripes,
Smoking our pipes,
Come marching home once more,
When the war is o'er.
When the war is o'er,
And our victory is won,
Then let's cheer up boys,
For our emblem so true
Our colors, the Red, White and Blue,
That have won our victory.
Let Old Glory proudly wave,
O'er the homes of our brave
And the land that's made us free,
Sweet land of Liberty,
When we soldiers come marching home again.

I have roamed o'er the wide world in quest of
    a guide,
Like the one who went down in the ocean's blue
    tide,
But my heart is still yearning for the spirit that
    fled,
While alone in my vigils hope's idol is dead.
The glory of young manhood has faded from
    view
And though year after year my sad life I renew
There's no balm in new friendship to charm
    away care.
No power in sweet music to lift my despair.

Though the bright whirl of fashion dulls senses
    of woe
Yet I'm haunted by lost love where'er I may go,
And while casts its shadow o'er my time-wrinkled
    brow,
There dwells in my sad soul young love's simple
    vow.
Though my kindred and friends, of life's early
    years
Are borne to the tomb midst sorrow and tears
Yet the pain for their absence is naught to com-
    pare
With the moan for lost love in the night of des-
    pair.
        Chorus.
I have passed through the last turn in long,
    weary life,
Have fought bravely each battle and won in each
    strife,
But the fierce storm of anguish that sweeps o'er
    my soul,
Gives no token of respite as the years onward
    roll.
Manhood's prime has elapsed, I'm fast turning
    gray,
While time and its mystery are circling away,
And though dim grows my vision yet a sight
    deeper far
Sees the light of the loved ones in hope's set-
    ting star.

MEMORIAL MONOGRAM.

By J. W. Evarts.

On this page, what can or should I write?
Not of frail things that quickly droop and die,
No transitory thoughts should I here indite,
No echoing vigils of times that withering lie.
Why speak of forms or flowers that face today,
Why laud fair fields that soon are dry and shorn,
Why talk of things death has laid away?
To wither and droop is brightest beauty born.
To passion's shrine no meed of praise is due.
To beauty's queen a heart of stone is given
Woes and strife, ambition's path lead through.
Wealth and power are by the tumults riven.
All things must perish as time's cycles turn,
All vital breath is quick to come and go.
Memory recoils from earth's ignoble urn,
Life's fitful sparks turn upward in its woes,
Who live for passion, dies as sorrow's slaves,
Who live for power, die mocked by they who
    mourn,
Who live for wealth, are honored most by knaves,
And self love by heartless hands are born.
What then, in life is worth a word of praise,
In earth's expanse, in depths below or skies
    above?
What then to repay the toil of life's dark days?
No answer comes if not in immortal love.

A VISION OF PARADISE.

By J. V. Evarts (Written in 1892.)

"Mr. Crow, what on earth does this mean?
Somebody is getting into this bed. It seems all
the devils in hell are let loose."

"Oh, no, Evarts, there is nothing unusual.
You must be dreaming. My arm may be touch-
ing you as I turn over."

"Arm nothing. Somebody is crawling in on
the back side. Dreaming! Dreaming! No, I'm
wide awake and sitting up, and there's a man

with a lantern just coming in."

"Lay down and sleep, Evarts. That terrible rain storm we had last night made you a little nervous. Take a good drink of this brandy; it will cure that chill you had today."

I partook of the brandy copiously, showing I was wide awake, and laid down again with no more consciousness until Mr. Crowe lit a lamp and called me at 5:30 the next morning for breakfast. While dressing, I related a vision the most real imaginable that came to me that night. One thing about Mr. Crowe, he was a very fine cook and breakfast was soon ready. We each took forty-one or more drops of brandy, and while eating, Mr. Crowe remarked to me that he would introduce me to a couple of his most congenial friends after breakfast. He gathered the leavings of the table into a platter and called "Elijah," "Job." "Come to your breakfast." Instantly the bed covers moved vigorously and Mr. Crowe raised the quilt and laid them back on the foot board, disclosing two monstrous reptiles, who viciously thrust out tongues seven or eight inches long, crawled to the door and ate their food. They then gave me a searching stare, moved slowly toward a big hole in the dirt wall of the house, looked back at me sharply and disappeared. A moment later, the head of one of the reptiles appeared at the mouth of the hole and took from Mr. Crow's hand a piece of fresh meat and returned. Then the other followed suit. In size, one was fully twelve feet long and four inches in diameter with a head about ten inches long, five inches broad and three inches thick. The other reptile was a trifle smaller, about seven feet long. In color, they resembled the rattle snake breed. What was very singular, was that when Mr. Crowe was alone in the house, the reptiles would come out of their dens and rub their heads in a caressing manner as if their feeling were responsive to his kindness to them.

John M. Crowe was in the Confederate service during the Civil War. He has been well known since that time in northern Texas, Indian Territory and Oklahoma, as a man of strict integrity, a good neighbor and a worthy citizen. In 1889, when Oklahoma was thrown open to settlement, Mr. Crowe and myself took homesteads about five miles south of where the small village of Yukon is now located. In September of that year, Mr. Crowe and I traveled over the Chickasaw Nation, enjoying, together, many days of hunting and fishing, enjoying out-door camp life when that country was a wilderness. Our destination was Suggsville in the heart of the notorious Picken county where Mr. Crowe owned and operated a cotton gin, a grist mill, a fairly good house, and farm machinery. I was shaking with ague when we arrived at Suggsville. The only medicine obtainable was arsenic, quinine and calomel and the abominable brandy from Fort Reno, Okla.

But no medicine was needed after the first night at Mr. Crowe's house. With two monstrous reptiles as bed fellows—whether the contact cured my malady, or intense fright did it, I cannot say—the demon of disease was cast out, leaving me spell-bound, as if in a hypnotic trance. Continually haunting me, was a man with a lantern. And in the wonderful vision the same man was showing me a most beautiful country and leading me into a vast ampitheatre filled with many thousands of finely dressed people. Among them he pointed to the speaker, who was Benjamin Franklin, explaining an apparatus which he called a pschycoscope, and which he had proven would accurately transmit thought from one planet to another.

I have no doubt but that Mr. Crowe will vouch for the simple truth of this narrative, and if questioned could give facts connected with his pet snakes. It would be well worth scientific inquiry.

LAND MONOPOLY.

By J. W. Evarts.

The Christian religion is a misnomer. Why? Because it strains at holy days, whereas Jesus was a Sabbath breaker. Because it meddles with personal liberty, whereas Jesus was a wine maker. Because it says morality will not save, whereas only the pure in heart shall see God.

Law is a misnomer. Why? Because it favors the rich and oppresses the poor, because it upholds land monopoly, while the poor are homeless and lacking bread. Because it incorporates seizures of the fruits of toil, while laborers are driven into vagrancy and crime. Presidents, martyrs and statesmen of all ages, sell themselves to the church for the price of the religious vote. In as much as special cohesive power accrues to protestant theology, wherein liars, thieves, perjurers, robbers and embezzlers flood in resistance to malicious laws.

That which nature bestows upon man is what nature possesses, previous to man—physical structure and intellect pre-expressing in nature.—J. W. Evarts.

By Benjamin F. Gilbert.

Go crazy, preacher, and to pale Cynthia howl,
And be answered by the screeching owl,
You make God hideous with your fearful hells,
For what it is and where it is you ne'er pretend
    to tell.

By J. B. Gilbert.

If I be a doctor, I must break my rest and stand
    the cold,
To obtain the shining gold.
If I be a lawyer, I must lie and cheat,
For an honest lawyer has no bread to eat.

CPSIA information can be obtained
at www.ICGtesting.com
Printed in the USA
BVHW041612210219
540827BV00024B/2796/P